1995

EDISON AT WORK
The Thomas A. Edison Laboratory

Edison at work in the Chemical Building shortly after it was built. The photograph is one of many taken by W. K. L. Dickson, the laboratory photographer who also played a leading role in the invention of the motion picture camera. This picture was taken in the late 1880's.

THE FAMOUS MUSEUM SERIES

EDISON
AT WORK

The Thomas A. Edison Laboratory
at West Orange, New Jersey

by DAVID W. HUTCHINGS

Illustrated with photographs

HASTINGS HOUSE, PUBLISHERS

NEW YORK

For Dorothy and Mel Shuttlesworth

Published simultaneously in Canada by
Saunders, of Toronto, Ltd. Don Mills, Ontario
SBN: 8038-1893-9

Library of Congress Catalog Card Number: 78-98058
Printed in the United States of America

Contents

ACKNOWLEDGMENTS   7

INTRODUCTION   9

1 THE LABORATORY EVOLVES   11

2 IMPROVEMENTS ON THE TELEGRAPH   21

3 THE PHONOGRAPH   29

4 IMPROVING THE TELEPHONE   37

5 THE INCANDESCENT LAMP   41

6 THE MOTION PICTURE CAMERA   49

7 THE KINETOSCOPE   56

8 THE BLACK MARIA   59

9 CARS AND BATTERIES   65

10 THE MACHINE SHOP   73

11 THE LIBRARY   79

TOURS AND VISITING HOURS   87

BIBLIOGRAPHY   89

INDEX   91

Note: The Thomas A. Edison Laboratory is listed in directories as the Edison National Historic Site.

Acknowledgments

I AM INDEBTED to a number of friends and advisors for their able assistance in the preparation of this book. At the Edison National Historic Site, Mr. Melvin Weig, Superintendent, Mrs. Henry Appleby, Management Assistant, and Mr. Norman R. Speiden, Curator, each read the manuscript offering their very helpful suggestions and corrections. Mrs. Robert McGuirk, archivist, and Mr. Harold Anderson, curator, were both generous with their time in searching out photographs and other data. My immediate associates at Edison, Historian John Heath and Park Guides John C. F. Coakley and Paul B. Kasakove, two men who knew Thomas A. Edison, have been helpful in many ways through discussions and reminiscences.

Writer Dorothy Shuttlesworth (Mrs. Melvin C. Shuttlesworth), with many books to her credit, edited each chapter and made many suggestions, and my wife

Esther not only helped with the text but also did numerous household chores which I should have done but could not because of work on this project.

My thanks to Simon and Schuster, Inc. for kind permission to quote from *A Million and One Nights* by Terry Ramsaye, and to The Edison Institute for permission to quote from *Menlo Park Reminiscences* by Francis Jehl.

Finally, I extend my deep appreciation to Mrs. Jean P. Colby, editor at Hastings House, for her excellent help and encouragement.

David W. Hutchings

Introduction

THE EDISON MUSEUM is located in the New Jersey town
of West Orange, a suburb of New York. Here in 1887,
Thomas Edison, newly famous as the inventor of the
electric light and power system, came to live in a hill-
side home and constructed his new laboratory in the
valley below.

Then forty years of age, Edison was to work here for
the remaining forty-four years of his life. From his creative mind, as well as from the hands of the skilled
artisans on his staff, were to evolve the first successful
motion picture cameras and commercial films, improved
phonographs with their cylinder and disc records, ore
milling machinery, better processes for Portland cement
manufacture, the new long-life alkaline storage battery,
and a host of other inventions important to the society
in which this great man lived.

The laboratory buildings still stand, a monument

9

and memorial to one of the most prolific and versatile inventors since Leonardo Da Vinci. In 1956 they were placed under the supervision of the National Park Service, United States Department of the Interior, and are now kin to many other famous historic sites across the nation as an important unit of the National Park System.

Guided tours take the visitor through the main buildings and into laboratories unchanged since Edison's death and the closing of his "invention factory" in 1931. The museum tells the story of the man who rose from itinerant newsboy to practical genius — the inventor who, during his adult years, was rated "the most useful American."

1

The Laboratory Evolves

ON A SUMMER DAY in the year 1931, a white-haired, white-clad man set aside a scientific magazine he had been reading, and rose from his simple desk. Taking off his lab coat, he hung it on the customary hook next to his chair, and strolled down the long aisle between the laboratory tables to the door. It has been said that at the time he was not feeling well and was going home. He then left the laboratory and the work on his final project. It is doubtful that he ever again spent much time there.

That man was Thomas Alva Edison, inventor. The place was the Chemical Building of his laboratory in West Orange, New Jersey. It was in these surroundings that he spent the last forty-four years of his life and when he died on October 18, 1931, his legacy to his own and future generations included many inventions that changed the lives of his fellowmen.

Edison had not lived all of his life in West Orange. Born in Milan, Ohio, he moved with his family seven years later to Port Huron, Michigan. Even as a small boy he revealed an amazing amount of patience, determination, and curiosity, constantly asking for explanations about things he noticed around the Edison home. At age six, he conducted one of his earliest known experiments when he sat on a nest of goose eggs for hours attempting to hatch the eggs as he had seen the mother goose do. On another occasion, when he was experimenting with fire, he accidentally burned down his father's barn.

Edison gathered together the necessary equipment for a chemical laboratory when he was nine. First housed in his bedroom, then in the basement of his home, his collection of chemicals, test tubes, and other working materials helped the young experimenter to lay the foundation for a knowledge of chemistry that would be invaluable to the inventor he was to become. This "hobby" was such a serious business with young Tom Edison that he would spend endless hours in the cellar, sometimes all day, studying the behavior of chemicals and gases, and trying to absorb the basic principles of a fascinating science.

By the time he was twelve, he had taken a job as a newsboy and candy merchant on the local railroad, thus earning money to buy additional chemicals from the town druggist. However, finding that his hours at home were much reduced by this new venture, young Edison moved his chemical laboratory into the baggage car of

View of the interior of Building 1 as it appeared in the 1930s, after Edison's death. The apparatus is for the testing of the alkaline storage batteries. *(See Chapter 10.)*

the train and proceeded with experiments when not hawking his wares.

As he approached the age of fifteen, Edison's interest in chemistry was somewhat eclipsed by his growing fascination with the telegraph and the mysteries of electricity. He had made his first telegraph set in his basement laboratory several years earlier. From 1862 to 1869, he was a telegraph operator. During his spare moments he carried on experiments that were mostly concerned with his trade. Like other enterprising young men of his time he was intrigued by many unsolved problems associated with his new mode of communication.

Moving from the Midwest to Boston, Edison left his job as telegraph operator so that he could devote all his time to improving telegraphic devices. Within a year of his arrival in Massachusetts he had moved on to New York City, where his knowledge and skill deeply involved him in the manufacture and sale of improved telegraphic stock tickers. Setting up a financially rewarding business in Newark, he found that his activities as combined owner, manager, and foreman in his new factory left him little time for experimenting.

By 1876, having never forgotten his main objective of being a successful inventor, Edison sold his business, took his accumulated fortune of about $300,000, and built his first real research laboratory at Menlo Park, New Jersey. The original two-story frame building was completed in January, 1876 but several months later, as the need became apparent, several small sheds were added, and in 1878 a library and office. A machine shop and power house were the final additions. With his time now solely devoted to inventing, Edison set a schedule of a minor invention every ten days and a major one every six months.

The next very successful ten years of the inventor's life made even larger facilities necessary. Calling upon his extensive experience with laboratory technique, Edison carefully planned the details of his new laboratory to be built in West Orange. While it was under construction in 1887, Edison wrote enthusiastically about the nature and purpose of the project:

> "My laboratory will soon be completed ... I will have the best equipped and largest laboratory extant, and the facilities incomparably superior to any other for rapid and cheap development of an invention, and working it up into commercial shape with models, patterns, and special machinery. In fact there is no similar institution in existence. We do our own castings ... and can build anything from a lady's watch to a locomotive."
>
> (LABORATORY NOTEBOOK, 1887)

The first buildings were of brick and wood construction, six in all. The main edifice, about 200 feet long and three stories high, contained Edison's combination office and laboratory, the machine shops and stock rooms, a music room, photography shop, drafting room, and offices for the managerial staff. Attached to this building, Five, was Building Six, the heating plant and powerhouse.

The remaining four buildings contained the specialized laboratories and shops: Building 1 — the Physics and Electrical Laboratory; Building 2 — the Chemical Laboratory; Building 3 — Chemical storage and pattern shop; Building 4 — The Metallurgical Laboratory. A small blacksmith shop and other outbuildings completed the original building complex.

Since that first laboratory in the basement of his Port Huron home, the inventor had come a long way.

The West Orange Laboratory as seen in a photograph taken about 1895. Building 5 is to the right; Building 1 and the Gate House in the foreground. Note the old trolley car which connected the town of Orange with Newark.

The Thomas A. Edison Laboratory as it appears today. The six original buildings are enclosed on three sides by the concrete factory installations, built between 1904 and 1916.

The Chemical Building remains much as it was when the inventor left there in 1931. From the entrance, a long aisle extends practically the length of the building. On either side are lab tables crowded with the tools, chemicals, and apparatus of experimentation.

Near the far end of the room are the table, scientific journals, and laboratory coat already mentioned.

One of Edison's techniques in his "invention factory" was to keep his assistants well supplied with everything they might need for inventing. Several cabinets in the chemical building still contain a wide variety of chemicals. *Photo: Courtesy of Thomas Cervasio*

In an adjoining room is another lab table on which rests a jar containing raw rubber extracted from the goldenrod plant. Edison's final project was to involve him and his aids in a search for rubber in plants native to North America. Searching for a domestic rubber supply, the experimenters tested over 17,000 plants,

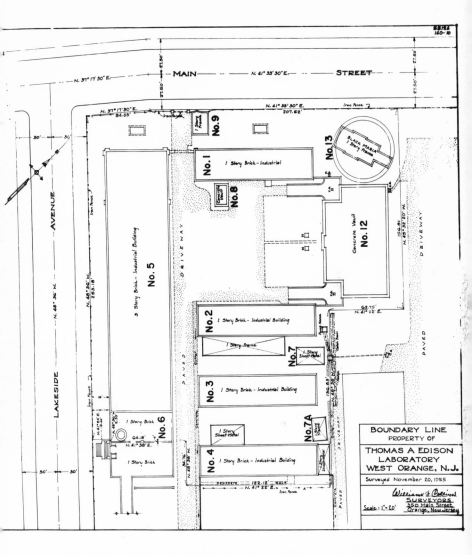

This 1955 surveyor's drawing indicates the position of the laboratory buildings at the corner of Main Street and Lakeside Avenue in West Orange, New Jersey. The entrance to the Museum is at the Gatehouse (No. 9) on Main Street. Guided tours move in a clockwise direction, starting in No. 1 building and terminating in No. 5. As tours are continuous, visitors can join the tour as they arrive at the site.

Edison's crude desk in his chemical laboratory. His lab coat hangs where he left it in the summer of 1931, and scientific journals of that summer remain on the desk. *Photo: Courtesy of Thomas Cervasio*

finding natural rubber in 1200 of them. Goldenrod was isolated as the best source as it gave a good yield, was a one season plant and was easily grown in just about any soil where rainfall was ample. It also could be mowed and reaped with machinery.

2

Improvements on the Telegraph

NOT ALL BUILDING interiors remain as they were when the laboratory was in operation. After the establishment of the Museum in the 1930's, the Electrical and Physics Building was chosen to exhibit various inventions and displays having to do with Edison's life.

Here the visitor can see a minutely detailed scale model of a mid-nineteenth century railroad engine, tender, and baggage car. It was while working on a train such as this that Edison came to know the telegraphers at stations along the route. One of them taught Edison how to be a telegraph operator.

In a display case near the train, a yellowing sheet of paper contains part of an actual message copied by him in 1868 in Boston, the last year he worked as a telegraph operator. Visitors remark about Edison's beautiful handwriting.

Possibly it was his mother who taught him his pen-
manship skills. We know that Edison's experience in
the Port Huron one room school was a failure. Tom began and ended his formal education at the age of eight.
His mother, suspecting her son to be gifted, but puzzled
by his lack of success in school, decided to tutor him at
home. For the next four years Edison was taught reading and writing, and was exposed to some of the world's
great literature. He particularly took to science books,
his interest in chemistry following. But it was in his
work with the telegraph that Edison's unusual education began to bring dividends, although not without
disappointments at first.

He turned to full-time inventing when he was 21.
Quitting his operator job, he applied himself to the
making of his first commercial invention — the electric
vote recorder, the predecessor of the modern voting
machine now being adopted in various legislative
houses in the United States and Europe. Ironically, law-
makers in Washington refused to buy it, claiming it
would not be practical. Two pictures of this machine
are in Building 6.

After this, Edison declared that he would never
again invent anything that was not commercially useful, and turned to improvements on the telegraph itself.
Over the next seven years, working mostly in Newark,
Edison patented more than one hundred inventions,
the majority in the telegraphic field. Many were improvements on the stock ticker and the gold indicator,
devices for transmitting the changes in stock and gold

The Electric Vote Recorder, Edison's first patented invention, created by the inventor when he was 21 years of age. Failure to find buyers moved Edison to vow he would never again spend time developing a device which was not practical.

prices from one office to others. Both these machines had been invented shortly before Edison arrived in Boston, but were imperfect. At times they printed wildly, transmitting meaningless figures from the central exchange to more than a hundred brokerage houses. When this happened, pandemonium broke loose among the thousands of brokers, speculators, and investors who spent their working day closely following the change in prices. Whenever a transmitting ticker broke down, linemen had to be sent running from the central exchange to the brokerage-receiving office in order to set the receiving devices at zero. Following the repair of the transmitter, it too was set at zero, and the ticker reactivated.

Edison saw the necessity of improving on this arrangement. Using his plentiful supply of intelligence and ingenuity, he invented and patented the unison-stop device, whereby all receiving instruments could automatically be returned to zero from the central transmitting office.

When Edison demonstrated this machine to Marshall Lefferts, president of Western Union, the inventor's thought was that the unison-stop device ought to be worth $5,000. Too nervous to even quote a figure,

The Universal Stock Printer with the keyboard and Edison's name plainly visible on the front. This and other improvements in the telegraphic field helped supply Edison with the funds to build his first large laboratory in Menlo Park.

Edison almost fainted when Lefferts asked him if he would accept $40,000! A framed painting hanging on the museum wall behind the telegraph exhibit shows the amazed Edison reacting to Lefferts' offer.

The importance of this invention to Edison's career as well as to the success of the stock ticker cannot be overestimated. Edison immediately became accepted as an important contributor to the telegraphic field. Within one year after this success he received an order for 1,200 stock tickers incorporating a number of his improvements. Further research in his own factory-laboratory in Newark resulted in the invention of the Universal Stock Printer. This was a transmitting device that came into general use in the major brokerage houses in both Europe and America. One of these machines can be seen in Building 1, and the remark often heard as visitors view it is that the machine resembles an early typewriter, as it has a keyboard of letters.

Yet all this was only a beginning to Edison's improvements in the field of telegraphy. Operators in the early 1870's were still restricted to sending one message at a time over a single wire. Edison knew that if he could manage to transmit several messages at a time on the same wire (multiplex telegraphy), he could save the telegraph industry millions of dollars.

He turned his attention to other things but a few years later again went to work on the multiplex. This time he began with the duplex and built on knowledge he had started to accumulate earlier while experimenting in Boston. With his customary determination and

hard work, he perfected the quadruplex the following year. Long after, he confessed that the problem of the quadruplex had been one of the most difficult and complicated he had ever solved.

The story is told that in the midst of these experiments Edison received a notice from the Newark city hall to pay his taxes promptly or a substantial fine would be added to the amount due. On the final day of the grace period, with less than an hour to closing time, he took his place at the end of a slow-moving line of taxpayers. As he waited, his mind turned again to the problems he was having with the complex mechanism of his proposed quadruplex. Suddenly he was at the window and the clerk was asking his name. The young inventor could not remember it! The clerk impatiently waved him aside and handled the next transaction. The closing hour arrived, the window slammed shut, and the dazed inventor was left with the penalty as well as the unpaid tax.

The quadruplex was not a single device but a complex arrangement of several that included relays of electromagnets, permanent magnets, current variation switches, and other regular telegraphic instruments and wires. A diagram of the arrangement is at the museum. However, in order to really appreciate it, a visitor should know something of the hard work Edison put into it and its value to the telegraph industry. Matthew Josephson,* recent biographer of Edison, stated that

---

Edison (McGraw-Hill Book Company, Inc., New York) 1959. p. 124.

The Repeating Telegraph — the machine which speeded up message transmission and also helped pave the way for the invention of the phonograph. Note the use of the disc paper on the left turntable.

the quadruplex was "one of the most important contributions to the telegraphic art." Over a thirty-year period, its use saved Western Union $20,000,000 in telegraph wire alone. As for the inventor, the sale of the rights to this invention helped pave the way for the erection of his laboratory at Menlo Park in 1876.

The Repeating Telegraph, another Edison invention that may be seen in Building 1, also played an eventful role in history. Many visitors find that this instrument reminds them of a modern tape recorder as it has two discs side by side, resting on a common chassis. Others say that it looks like a two-turntable record player. Actually the two brass discs *are* turntables. Suspended over each, as the arm of a phonograph might be, is a similar arm with a needle at the end. On the left turntable, this needle rests on a paper disc that must have been the first type of disc record. This invention was a help to operators as the left-hand part automatically inscribed the dots and dashes of Morse-coded messages

on the paper disc.* At the end of the message, the operator merely transferred the disc to the other turntable
where another needle "picked up" the impulses by passing over the Morse indentations on the disc, thus transmitting the message to the next station. All this was
done automatically six to eight times faster than an
average-speed operator could do the job manually.

In experimenting with the repeating telegraph, Edison noticed that the transmitting side, when switched
to extreme high speed, gave off "indistinct muttering"
sounds, "almost human." Edison pondered this new development. An idea was taking form in his amazing
mind of a machine that would reproduce the sound of
the human voice — the phonograph.

---

*The Morse code, named after its inventor, consists of one or more
 dots or dashes, or a particular combination of the two, for each
 letter of the alphabet as well as for numbers Ex. "A" equals ·-,
 and B equals -···, C equals -··-·, etc.

3

The Phonograph

THE CRAFTSMAN who constructed the first record player in the world did not understand how it was going to work. That man was John Kruesi, former Swiss clockmaker, who in 1877 was in the employ of Thomas Edison. Making clocks was not Kruesi's only skill. A good thinker, an improviser, and with a background of work in various crafts in Europe, he could make just about any kind of machine or instrument that was described to him.

Kruesi was an example of the kind of skilled craftsmen that Edison gathered around himself from the time he opened his first factory in Newark. When the inventor gave Kruesi the plans for the first phonograph, they were accepted without question. But during the two weeks that he was working on the machine, the clockmaker's curiosity got the better of him and he asked Edison what the invention was meant to do. Told that the machine was supposed to talk, Kruesi thought the idea ridiculous. However, being one of Edison's most faithful assistants, he continued with his task. When he had completed the mysterious machine, Edison placed it on a table in his workshop, drew up a chair, and gathered his laboratory staff around him.

The first record was a piece of tinfoil that was wrapped around a metal cylinder. There was a transmitter, or dictating part, within which was a diaphragm connected to a needle or stylus. The needle was located on one side of the cylinder, while a similar mechanism on the other side acted as a reproducer. In order to channel the sound waves from his voice into the diaphragm, Edison made a megaphone from a piece of cardboard and installed it on the dictating side of the phonograph. His theory was that the sound of the human voice would cause the diaphragm to vibrate, and this in turn would activate the needle, causing it to make indentations on the tinfoil. A crank on the right of the machine would enable the operator to move the cylinder when he talked or shouted into the mouthpiece.

As Edison made the preliminary adjustments, his men good-naturedly kidded him about the remote possibilities for the success of the invention. Edison made no reply, and years later he admitted that at the time he had not been completely confident himself. He started turning the crank with seeming assurance, however, and at the same time he slowly shouted into the megaphone the words of the familiar rhyme —

Mary had a little lamb,
Its fleece was white as snow,
And everywhere that Mary went,
The lamb was sure to go.

Readers can imagine the effect this recitation had on the rough and ready men of Edison's laboratory. They joked and laughed, taunting their leader, betting him cigars that the contraption would not function, even suggesting that their mentor had worked so hard he was beginning to show signs of mental strain!

Edison paid little heed to their remarks. He had learned early to ignore people who offered only criticism instead of constructive suggestions.

At first try, the tinfoil tore before the verse was completed. So calmly Edison started over and this time completed the message. It was truly an odd one for so dramatic a step in the development of a new communication medium! Then he removed the megaphone from its dictating side and placed it opposite on the reproducer. Next, after returning the cylinder to the original position and adjusting the reproducing needle on the tinfoil indentations, he again started turning the crank. This moved the cylinder forward once more.

The men had now quieted down and were eagerly leaning over Edison as he, in turn, huddled over his invention. Into the silence of that room came the sound of Edison's voice, reproduced quite perfectly, reciting the nursery rhyme. For the first time in the history of mankind the human voice had been successfully recorded and reproduced.

The original tinfoil phonograph invented by Thomas A. Edison in the autumn of 1877. This phonograph may be seen at the Thomas A. Edison Laboratory.

Gasps of surprise came from the men. The machine's maker, Kruesi, exclaimed in his native Swiss, "My God in Heaven!" Edison himself was amazed and shocked. Later he commented that he did not know whether to be happy or sad, for he felt inventions that worked the first time sometimes developed many problems later.

The remainder of that day, December 6, 1877, saw the same men who had mocked the inventor eagerly seeking their turn to try out the new device. It was demonstrated the next morning in New York City to the amazed staff of the *Scientific American* magazine and to the press. The news spread quickly across the nation that the eccentric inventor from New Jersey had invented a "phonograph." Today, this first record player is on display in Building 1 at the Edison Laboratory Museum.

After this initial activity, Edison set aside the development of the phonograph to turn his attention to electric lighting and power. In fact, it was not until the move to the West Orange Laboratory in 1887 that he proceeded to develop the phonograph. Once Edison was established there the phonograph became big business and opened up vast related fields of endeavor.

With improved models of 1887 and 1888, the cylinder itself was reduced in size, the tinfoil was replaced by durable wax cylinder records, and an electric motor was introduced, thus replacing the primitive crank. The introduction of stethoscope-like tubes for the ears improved the listener's ability to hear records. A transmitting speaking tube did away with the megaphone.

The Type M phonograph of 1890, which also is on display at the museum, reveals the inventor's practical mind. He literally piped the sound out of the machine. Thirteen faucets on the pipe from the reproducer actually allowed thirteen people to listen at the same time. Soon the amplifying trumpet or horn made the Type M phonograph obsolete.

One of the earliest machines to use the trumpet was the Edison Home Phonograph. First developed in 1896, the instrument's large horn was flower-shaped, and it was given the name "Morning-glory." This and subsequent cylinder phonographs developed in West Orange all had spring-wound motors and sapphire needles. And they played either the two-minute black records, or, after 1913, the improved four minute celluloid Blue Amberol.

Edison was reluctant to develop disc records. However, his claim that the cylinders were better had little effect on the growing market for discs. Finally, with other manufacturers having such great success with the disc, Edison started production of his version in 1913.

Meanwhile, Edison had another improvement under way. Two years before, his company had come out with an extremely high-quality machine known as the Concert or Opera Phonograph. Unlike the previous cylinder models, the Concert had a revolving trumpet that could be used, to some degree, to control the volume. Inasmuch as all of these early Edison record players were completely mechanical, there was no other volume control.

Today the thickness of Edison disc records amazes visitors at the Edison Laboratory Museum, accustomed as they are to the thin discs of the last 40 years. The core of the Edison disc was made of compressed sawdust-like wood with other substances blended in to give the black color. The surface recording material was bakelite, one of the world's earliest plastics. Unbreakable and of high quality, these discs became world famous.

In those days, noted musicians were often seen entering the Edison studios for a recording session. Edison, himself, was said to have passed judgment on all recordings before they were released.

Nowadays it is difficult for people to appreciate the impact of the phonograph on the world at the turn of the century. To Edison, it was the invention he loved

The Edison Home Phonograph with accompanying Morningglory
Horn is studied by a young visitor to the Edison Laboratory. This
was one of the earliest cylinder phonographs. Note the wooden
cabinet. The drawers are especially made to store cylinder records.
Photo: Courtesy of Thomas Cervasio

best. He produced it when he was little known, and it brought him international fame. To a world devoid of the type of home entertainment so common to us now, the phonograph was a delight and source of amusement surpassing any previous musical machine. Even though it was a far cry from today's stereo and hi-fi, the early record player paved the way for the multitudinous sounds of the present.

4

Improving the Telephone

In Building 1 of the Edison Laboratory, an old wooden telephone rests between several of his telegraphic inventions. A boxlike affair, less than a foot square, it has a front cover that stands open. A large bell with hammer rests on its top; coils and wire are inside. A telephone receiver stands below, but there is no sign of a transmitter. Pasted inside the open door, a yellow, faded card reads —

> *Mr. Thomas A. Edison*
>   A very happy Birthday!
> This telephone invented by you in 1877
> was in use at North Columbia, Nevada County,
> California, in 1878 on a 60 mile long
> distance telephone line.
>   Sincerely,
>   (signed) J. A. Wolff
> Grass Valley, Calif.
> 1-31-31

Everyone knows that Alexander Graham Bell invented the telephone. Edison himself admitted this. Yet our telephone today is different in many important ways from the one invented by Bell in 1876. In Bell's machine, one piece acted as both receiver and transmitter. Tests made with this device from New York City to Newark gave decidedly unfavorable results. The message could not be transmitted clearly because of interfering noises from various sources.

Bell patented his telephone in February, 1876, but, in spite of the remarkable nature of the invention, many wealthy people refused to buy or even to help finance it. William Orton of Western Union, for example, turned down Bell's offer to sell it with the remark, "What can we do with such an electrical toy?" However, after Bell gave a fairly successful demonstration of the telephone during the Philadelphia Centennial Exposition in July, other inventors were lured into the field, all attempting to make the instrument really practical. One such newcomer was Edison.

Following Bell's success in Philadelphia, Orton contacted Edison and asked him to take on the job of improving the strange device. Western Union was growing worried about possible competition and if Edison could make a breakthrough with a practical long-distance instrument, the Western Union management would be in a position to negotiate a good settlement with Bell.

Actually, this was by no means a new field to Edison. During the previous year, he and a number of other inventors had been experimenting independently of each other with acoustic telegraphy, a device that evolved quite naturally from intensive work with the telegraph. It had come a long way since Morse developed the instrument and technique in the 1840's, and Edison's role, as we have seen, was a very important one.

While reading about the activities of European inventors with the telephone, Edison had come across the experiments of a German inventor, one J. P. Reis of Frankfurt, who had made and demonstrated a primitive wood telephone in 1861.

After studying detailed reports on the Reis machine, Edison constructed a copy of it himself, and closely observed its operation. These labors led to his making a device for measuring sound waves and patenting it in June, 1876. In recent years, experiments with this Edison invention have shown it actually capable of transmitting speech, but Edison had never realized its true possibilities partly because of his poor hearing. Therefore, it was never patented as a telephone.

With Orton's request to pursue the telephone research further, Edison took up where he had left off. Working from the autumn of 1876 to January, 1877, he developed a separate transmitter capable of conveying articulated sentences over wires.

One year later, Edison patented a carbon button transmitter. The carbon button part was made from lamp-black scraped from pieces of lamp-chimney glass. In conjunction with other parts of the transmitter, the carbon button acted as an electric valve, enabling current to be increased or decreased as desired.

In March 1878, successful tests were made on a line stretching from New York to Philadelphia. The results were excellent, and the general feeling among those who observed the tests was that Edison had "liberated" the telephone. This success set the pattern for the type of machine that was to be used for the following fifty years.

The essential differences between Bell's telephone and Edison's centered around the transmitting of the sound waves. Bell's telephone sent sound vibrations against a diaphragm connected to an electro-magnet. In turn, these vibrations of the diaphragm sent very weak electrical impulses, or sound waves, to the electromagnet at the receiving end. This caused the receiving diaphragm to vibrate identically, imitating the sound of the person speaking. With Edison's improvements, a closed circuit was used with a constant flow of varying current provided by batteries. The sound waves actuated an electric valve, commonly known as an induction coil, allowing for the passage of current of any strength desired, thus making possible long-distance transmission of the sound of the speaking voice.

All modern telephone lines use the Edison improvements, including the varying electrical current with the induction coil. And all modern phones use the Bell receiver coupled with the Edison transmitter. In other words, today we actually talk into a transmitter of Edison's creation and listen through a Bell receiver.

Thus, though Edison did not invent the telephone, he did turn it into a workable device that revolutionized the field of communications. His early model well deserves its place of honor in the Museum.

5

The Incandescent Lamp

As a visitor enters the library of the Edison laboratory complex, his glance is drawn to a ten-foot, cream-white statue of a boyish form seated on the top of a gas street lamp of bygone times. The figure — winged and angelic — is triumphantly holding aloft a lighted electric bulb. This is no ordinary electric light; it was made in the 1880's and is one of the earliest commercial light bulbs ever produced. The sculptured marble statue might appropriately be labeled, "The triumph of the electric light."

The antique light that is being held high has a filament, plainly visible through the clear glass which is longer than those used today. It is in the shape of an inverted U and is constructed of Japanese bamboo. How the great inventor and his staff arrived at the use of bamboo and invented the first incandescent lamp makes an interesting story.

It was characteristic of the human dynamo that was Thomas A. Edison to have several projects in operation at the same time. Even his sleep was arranged to promote the longest hours of labor possible for a human frame. And from July 1876 to July 1878, with his staff, he was busy with the telephone, the phonograph, and improved telegraphic devices, as well as with preliminary testing of materials for incandescent lighting.

By this time Edison's reputation had grown greatly. More and more the inventor was being sought by learned men of his time. In the summer of 1878, he was invited to accompany a scientific expedition to Wyoming to observe an eclipse of the sun, and also to test another of his inventions — a tasimeter for measuring heat transmitted through the far reaches of space. George F. Barker, a professor at the University of Pennsylvania, who had a hand in arranging this trip, later took Edison to Ansonia, Connecticut, to see experiments in arc lighting. During this journey he suggested that Edison try to subdivide the electric light, to see if it was possible to have the power in small units, like gas.

Edison worked steadily on this idea and soon determined that, to be practical, an incandescent light should give high quality light for several hundred hours at a reasonable cost. The bulbs themselves would have to be inexpensive, yet very durable.

Further experiments indicated to the inventor that the essential components of such a lamp would include a hair-like carbonized filament of high electrical resistance. This was to be located in a bulb from which the air had been evacuated, since the lamp would not burn out as the filament heated up if the oxygen was eliminated in both filament and bulb.

On October 21, 1879, after many attempts with other materials, Edison and his staff succeeded in keeping a lamp with a simple carbonized cotton sewing-thread filament glowing for about forty hours.

One of the laboratory assistants at that time was a young man named Francis Jehl, who later became a leading European electrical engineer. In 1937, he published his recollections of just what had happened at Menlo Park during those October days and nights as scientific history was made. He recorded that it took ten hours on Sunday, the nineteenth, just to remove air from the bulb. Finally, at about eight o'clock in the evening the lamp was turned on. Jehl relates —

> That Sunday night, long after the other men had gone, Edison and I kept a deathwatch to note any convulsions or other last symptoms the lamp might give when expiring. The lamp, however, did not expire! In the morning we were relieved by Batchelor, Upton, and Force. The lamp continued to burn brilliantly all that day, passing the twenty-four hour mark. We were stirred with hope as each hour passed, more and more convinced of progress. Bets were made and general good humor existed all around ... During the night between the 20th and 21st, Edison, judging from the appearance of the lamp still burning without flaw, seemed satisfied that the first solid foundation of the future of electric

lighting had now been laid. The lamp held out hero-
ically that night and the following day until, between
one and two o'clock in the afternoon of Tuesday,
October 21, 1879, it had attained more than forty
hours of life.*

Edison and his men were sure they had developed
the first successful and practical electric light but realized their task was far from finished. They continued
to look for a filament that would glow longer and be
more durable.

Great progress was made with carbonized paper.
Several hundred such lamps were produced, the latter
ones reaching lifetimes of over 400 hours. With them
it was possible to put on an exciting exhibit on New
Year's Eve, 1879. Lighted bulbs were stretched on wires
both inside and outside the laboratory, as special trains
on the Pennsylvania Railroad brought over three thousand visitors to view this new phenomena.

But the inventor still was not satisfied. He was never
content with a job until it was done perfectly. Hence
the staff at Menlo proceeded to carbonize just about
everything they could get their hands on: tissue paper,
cardboard, twine, thread, various woods, tars and resins,
grasses, and, all told, over six thousand different species
of vegetable fibers alone. During this activity Edison
chanced to pick up one of the ordinary palm-leaf fans
with bamboo binding that were popular in those days,
Soon this bamboo material also was tested. The result

---

*Quoted from *Menlo Park Reminiscences*, by Francis Jehl.

was so successful that a man was quickly dispatched to Japan to obtain a supply of the most suitable bamboo. With this the first commercial electric lights were born!

Now a dramatic result had been achieved. But it was still only a beginning. Edison not only created the incandescent light but, assisted by his ever faithful staff, went on to develop whole electric power and lighting systems: sockets, fuses, wires, cables, switches, meters, and new improved dynamos. Display cases in Building 1 contain samples of some of the smaller electrical components mentioned. Even though they date from the early 1880's, similarities to their modern counterparts are readily apparent. Only a few feet away from these display cases is a six-foot high 1880 Edison dynamo which for some reason he nicknamed "The Long-waisted Mary-Ann." Edison's aide and mathematician, Francis Upton, played an important role assisting the inventor to produce this improved dynamo. Tests revealed it to be more than twice as efficient as any previously made dynamo. Edison was now ready to try out the whole power system in a commercial operation.

In the spring of 1880, a contract for an electric light installation was signed. The revolutionary bamboo filament lamps were tried out on an ocean steamer, the S. S. *Columbia,* that was sailing from San Francisco to New York around Cape Horn. Several hundred lamps were installed on the vessel, and not one burned out on the entire trip.

The "Long-waisted Mary-Ann" dynamo. This "Z" type dynamo developed by Edison in 1879 had an efficiency of 90%. The theoretical limit of dynamo efficiency, according to Electrical Science at that time, was 50%.

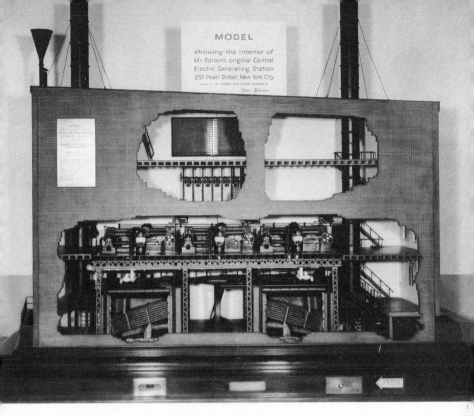

A scale model of Edison's original commercial station for generating current for incandescent light and electric power. Located at 257 Pearl Street in New York City, this station commenced operation on September 4, 1882.

In 1882 the U.S.A.'s first city central-power station was built on Pearl Street in downtown New York. Ten city blocks were lighted electrically in this experiment. It succeeded, and other cities across the nation soon followed that example. An operable scale model of the Pearl Street Station, one made for the St. Louis World's Fair of 1904, is now on exhibit at the Edison Museum. With its moving parts, it is a great aid to all who observe it closely in understanding the basic principles of electric generation.

Mr. and Mrs. Thomas A. Edison photographed in the Chemical Building in 1906.

6

The Motion Picture Camera

"I AM EXPERIMENTING upon an instrument which does for the eye what the phonograph does for the ear." So wrote Edison as he filed a caveat on his first motion picture machine.* (A caveat was an official notice to the United States Patent Office that work had started on an invention and that no patent should be granted to anyone else without allowing the caveat holder the opportunity to challenge the granting of that patent.)

The time was October 1888, and Edison had been in his laboratory at West Orange almost a year. Many changes had been made by the inventor since the tragic time in 1884 when his young wife had died at Menlo Park. Not only had he moved out of his laboratory there, but he had married again, had bought a luxurious home in West Orange, and then had built nearby the finest private industrial research laboratory in the world.

---

*Caveat 110; filed October 17, 1888, Orange, N.J.

Right after moving in, Edison returned to the invention he best loved — the phonograph, and started improving it. At the same time, in keeping with his policy of having several projects going at once, he began to search for a practical means of producing a motion picture machine.

After several months of secret endeavors, he filed the caveat with the patent office. A photostatic copy of this document is in one of the display cases in Building 1 of the Museum. And the visitor who takes the time to observe it closely will note a short comment at the top of the first page:

> "Seeley   Rush this   I am getting good
>   results.
>
>   Edison"

Edison also stated in the caveat that this would be an instrument for the purpose of recording and reproducing things in motion, "and in such a form as to be both cheap, practical and convenient." In this way Edison and his staff were attempting to make a breakthrough in a field in which several other men had been working for some time without much success.

One of the earliest attempts at making movies had been carried out by a Frenchman, Plateau, in the late 1700's. His device was called a Phenakistoscope and produced an illusion of motion. This toy was the forerunner of the zoetrope or "wheel of life" machine which consisted of a series of consecutive drawings, each slightly different from those before and after it. They were so arranged in a series that when they were passed or flipped rapidly before the eye, the viewer received the impression of motion.

The basic principles of the illusion of motion given by these machines was established by two later experimenters — Prof. E. J. Marey in France and Eadweard Muybridge in the United States. Working during the 1870s and 80's, these men proved that persistance of vision was an important quality of the human eye: when an image is impressed on the human retina, it remains for a period of from one-tenth to one-seventh of a second, the exact time varying according to the particular make-up of an individual and to the intensity of the light.

Marey and Muybridge both centered their projects around the zoetrope. The invention of the camera in the 1840's, however, advanced the realism of the zoetrope pictures tremendously, so photographic experiments comprised the bulk of the work done by those two men. For example, Muybridge, using sensitive wet plates and many cameras, took pictures of various animals in motion. Then, in 1886, he visited Edison and demonstrated these primitive motion pictures. Although there were various drawbacks to the method, Edison was evidently impressed. A number of years later when speaking of his work in motion pictures he referred to Marey and Muybridge as his forerunners. Incidentally, one of the drawbacks to making motion pictures prior to Edison's improvements can be appreciated by noting that if Muybridge had wanted to make motion pictures of a trotting horse for one full minute of action, he would have needed 720 separate cameras!

The approach used by Edison introduced something new. If the cylinder worked with the phonograph, why not with motion pictures? He arranged to have multiple photographs arranged spirally on a cylinder rather than on a wheel as in the zoetrope. The cylinder itself was originally covered with a coarse-grained, highly sensitized film. It was both a camera and a viewer as is evidenced by the wording of the caveat:

> The invention consists in photographing continuously a series of pictures occurring at intervals which intervals are greater than eight per second, and photographing these series of pictures in a continuous spiral on a cylinder or plate in the same manner as sound is recorded on the phonograph. At the instant the chemical action (photographing) on the cylinder takes place the cylinder is at rest and is only advanced in rotation a single step which motion takes place while the light is cut off by a shutter.*

One of these cylinders is in a display case in Building 1 of the Museum. The pictures on it, in spiral form, are very small. The image is about $\frac{1}{16}$ of an inch and is of a man going through the motions of waving his arms.

When someone wanted to view the picture on a cylinder, the photographic recording device was removed and a microscopic stand substituted. One hundred and eighty photographs for each revolution of the

---

*Op. cit. *Caveat 110.*

cylinder allowed about forty-two thousand pictures for the entire sequence. They would be displayed at a rate of twenty-five per second, allowing a movie of about twenty-eight minutes duration to be made. By connecting this machine with phonograph recordings, Edison with his great vision surmised that it might be possible in the future to "see and hear a whole opera as perfectly as if actually present although the actual performance may have taken place years before."

At about the same time that Edison was developing that first movie machine, which he called a "Kinetograph-Kinetoscope," another inventor George Eastman and his aids were further improving the new celluloid film. They gave their product the name Kodak. Hearing of these developments, Edison envisaged a move away from cylinders to strip film fed automatically to a shutter. Spurring the Eastman experts on to make a highly sensitized, fine-grained film in fifty-foot lengths, the inventor thought through a plan for this new type of camera.

His first modern motion picture machine, known as the Strip Kinetograph of 1889, is on display at the Edison Museum. It is located adjacent to the early cylinders, notebooks, and the caveat. The original cover, black and boxlike, has been replaced with a top of transparent plastic so that visitors may see the mechanical features of this marvelous invention.

Essentially, it consists of a feed reel and a take-up reel, separated by a shutter. The strip film was gathered on the feed reel, with two small electric motors so ar-

The world's first motion picture camera using strip film, Edison's 1889 Strip Kinetograph. This original machine, which employed horizontal rather than vertical film strips, is on display at Edison's laboratory.

ranged as to feed the film to the shutter, stop the film intermittently as the shutter was moved, and take up the film on a second reel. Involved in the heart of the machine was a sprocket wheel designed to keep the moving and stopping film perfectly synchronized with the other operations. The camera could be adjusted to take from twenty to forty pictures per second on nineteen millimeter (¾") film. Each circular picture was one-half inch in diameter.

Edison drew up the plans for this machine in the early summer of 1889, then dashed off to the Paris Exposition, leaving the project in the hands of W. K. L. Dickson, his chief assistant. Upon returning from Europe several weeks later, Edison was given a demonstration of the camera in a darkened room of one of the laboratory buildings. Dickson's later description of this event is reported by Terry Ramsaye in *A Million and One Nights*:

> The crowning point of realism was attained on the occasion of Mr. Edison's return from the Paris Exposition of 1889, when Mr. Dickson himself stepped out on the screen, raised his hat and smiled, while uttering the words of greeting, "Good morning, Mr. Edison, glad to see you back. I hope you are satisfied with the kineto-phonograph."

Dickson and his men had rigged up a special phonograph recording made at the time the film of Dickson was taken, and they had the machines synchronized. This was really a first in "Talking pictures!"

In 1890, an improved camera further aided in speeding the way to the first commercial movies, which were released in 1893, but the fact is that the strip-kinetograph of 1889 was really the first successful movie camera. It made possible the industry that became one of the commercial giants of the 20th century, and was to bring enjoyment and entertainment to people all over the world.

7

The Kinetoscope

ANOTHER EDISON invention closely related to the motion picture camera was the Kinetoscope. It came into general use in 1894, allowing the early Edison movies to be shown commercially for the first time. However, there is reason to believe that the first primitive kinetoscope, or movie-viewing machine, was created in 1889, and was used to show the earliest movies made on the kinetograph.

A simulated kinetoscope of the 1894 type is exhibited in Building 1. It is a rectangular wooden cabinet about four feet high with sides approximately two feet in length, and a peep-hole at the top. A step on the front, one foot above the floor, is for the children.

Although Edison had given some attention to the idea of projecting motion pictures onto a screen, he evidently discarded it in 1891. In his caveat for the 1889 camera, he mentioned a possible projector and a white

The Broadway Kinetoscope Parlor is seen in this advertising drawing of 1894. The early movies were seen by looking in the eye slot
on top of the machine. Each show cost five cents and lasted about
forty seconds.

screen. But there was much jerkiness in the early
movies and the projecting apparatus only made the
situation worse. The type of projector that we are familiar with today finally made its appearance in 1896,
but Armat, not Edison, was the inventor.

The Edison kinetoscope would probably never have
made any contribution to the development of the cin-
ema arts if it had not been for some friends of the inventor who persuaded him to display the machine to
the public at the Chicago Exposition of 1893. Although
none of the machines ever got to the fair, as they were
not completed in time, some associates saw great possibilities in the kinetoscope. Frank Gannon and Norman
C. Raff formed the Kinetoscope Company, which purchased a number of these peep-show machines, and
opened up Kinetoscope Parlors in various American
cities. These were a great success until the advent of

the screen-type projector in 1896. Contemporary newspaper accounts mentioned the success of the Broadway Kinetoscope Parlor, stating that on opening day, crowds waited in long lines all day and half the night to see pictures that had an average length of forty seconds. Crowds were also drawn to this new invention in other cities, including London and Paris.

The Edison peep-show phase of motion pictures was short-lived, passing into history as swiftly as it had entered. Yet its importance cannot be overestimated. An increased interest in the movies developed from the public's awareness of these first commercial showings. The next phase, the invention of the projector, "at last brought the shadow art-science before the world in full development."*

---

*Quigley, Martin, Jr., *Magic Shadows* (Georgetown University Press, Washington, D.C. 1948) p. 138.

8

The Black Maria

THE WORLD'S FIRST motion picture studio, the Black Maria,* was a strange, slapdash affair about the size of a very small bungalow. It was designed and built in 1893, so that the sun's rays would illuminate the subjects being filmed. Edison's original kinetographs had serious drawbacks: the film was so slow that only direct sunlight was bright enough to etch pictures on it, and outdoor light reflections were a handicap. The inside walls of this first studio were black, helping to eliminate reflections, and at the same time heightening the contrast between the actors and their background.

A replica of the Black Maria exists today at the Edison Museum. Because of its unusual architecture and the fact that it is located just a few feet from the street,

---

*The name was not Edison's creation although he seems to have approved of it. Supposedly it was the studio builders' joke that it looked like a policemen's paddy wagon, then known as the "Black Maria." The name stuck.

the building naturally draws the attention of passersby and visitors alike. The black, tarpaper-covered exterior no doubt contributes to its being one of the ugliest buildings in West Orange. But attractiveness was not a necessity of Edison inventions.

The original Black Maria was located several yards east of the laboratories where factory buildings now stand. It was about 50 feet long, 20 feet wide, and 18 high. Having an irregular oblong shape and a sharply sloping roof with hinges on the bottom edge, the entire structure could be revolved so as to capture the sun's rays throughout the day. The hinged portion was connected to a block and tackle by a stout rope, thus enabling men to crank the winch and open the roof. The center of the building swiveled on a pivot as wheels at each corner rode a circular track.

During the few years of its use, the original Black Maria underwent various changes. Some areas were shortened and others lengthened, but essentially the overall shape and appearance remained about the same. For all its historic importance to us today, the men associated with its use and purpose saw it as just a tar-paper-covered shack in which to make movies, and not anything more. Those early film pioneers had no block-long modern studios to compare their humble building with, nor could they draw on million dollar expense accounts to pay for their primary movies of thirty or forty seconds duration. To the contrary, the exact cost of the original Black Maria was $637.67! A good hurricane wind probably could have destroyed it.

The "Black Maria" — the world's first motion picture studio was erected in 1893 on the grounds of Edison's Laboratory in West Orange. A reconstruction of this building was erected in 1954 only a short distance from the site of the original.

In this respect as well as others, the replica is not the same. Built in 1954 at a cost of $25,000, the "copy" has the roof that can be opened and is revolvable. In short, it could be used to make movies just as its namesake was. From the outside, it also looks similar, and the inside is painted black. But there the resemblance stops. Built of sturdy timbers, a floor of polished hardwood supplemented by steel girders, heated as well as air-conditioned, the modern structure is designed to last for many years and so fulfill the purpose described on a plaque on the side of the building:

THIS BUILDING IS A REPLICA OF THE
ORIGINAL "BLACK MARIA," THE WORLD'S FIRST
MOTION PICTURE STUDIO
DEDICATED TO THE MEMORY OF
THOMAS ALVA EDISON
THE FOUNDER OF THE
MOTION PICTURE INDUSTRY
SEPTEMBER 22, 1954

Many famous people came to Edison's laboratory
to perform in this studio: Annie Oakley, Buffalo Bill,
some Sioux Indians, Gentleman Jim Corbett, and
Bronco Billy Anderson, to name a few. Jim Corbett as-
serted that it was the hottest and most cramped place
he had ever boxed in. While hot in summer, it was also
uncomfortable in winter. Terry Ramsaye, one of the
most illustrious historians of the motion pictures, claims
that the first star and studio troubles may have begun
with Edison's Black Maria. The following excerpt from
a letter written by Frank Gannon to W. E. Gilmore,
Edison's general manager, states:

> I was out there yesterday with a party to be taken
> for the Kinetoscope, but had great difficulty in per-
> suading them to go into the theatre (Black Maria) in
> their thin silk costumes, as it was just like going out
> into an open field in midwinter. We had to keep
> them there at least an hour, and if some of them do
> not take cold and die, I shall be agreeably surprised.
> I was informed that the part of the roof which raises
> was stuck, so that it could not be lowered. If it could
> have been closed, and a fire in the stove during re-
> hearsal, and then opened when ready to take the

scene, no complaint would have been made. Two or
three subjects which we have endeavored to secure
have absolutely refused to go out there, as they have
learned from others the true condition of the place.*

Sometime around 1903, the Black Maria disappeared.
If any record of its passing exists, it has not come to
light. It is known that more advanced and permanent
studios were built about this time in the Bronx and in
Manhattan. Glass-roofed buildings, both spacious and
heated, helped to bring more comfortable working conditions to the new movie industry.

Although the original movie studio is gone, that is
not true of some of the early film gems made in that
now famous structure. It has been the practice at the
Edison Museum to show two or three of these films to
visitors. Where are they shown? Right in the replica of
the Black Maria, which now serves as a theater — a
fitting memorial to the inventor of the modern motion
picture industry.

*Ramsaye, Terry, *A Million and One Nights*, p. 253.

Thomas A. Edison with a friend in his new 1911 Detroit Electric. This same car may be seen at the Thomas A. Edison Laboratory.

9

Cars and Batteries

VISITORS TO THE Edison Museum, particularly young people, are usually surprised to find antique cars exhibited. Three of these are electric cars manufactured between 1900 and 1915. The fourth is a 1922 Model T Ford, powered by a four-cylinder gasoline engine.

The oldest of the electrics is located in Building 1. The term "horseless carriage" could easily apply to this car. It is a 1902 Stanhope Locomobile with a small chaise borne on four oversized bicycle-type wheels with old pneumatic tires, and a large cushioned seat. A box-like area directly behind the seat contains a 21-cell storage battery* to provide the current for the motor.

---

*A storage cell is a rectangular affair containing two different metallic elements immersed in a conducting solution called the electrolyte. The chemical materials interact with each other and give off an electric current. A battery is a collection of two or more cells connected together.

The electric car's development was connected directly to improvements in the storage battery and the electric dynamo. Work progressed very rapidly in both these fields during the 1880's. In 1893, the first battery-powered electric car became a reality, and by 1900, the electrics were giving the older steam-type cars serious competition. These developments, of course, were before the gasoline-engine car was ready for production.

The battery used in the early electrics was the lead-acid make, the only type of storage battery available at that time. It had weaknesses. Not only did it leak and corrode, it had to be recharged frequently, and on the whole was short-lived. Recharging storage batteries took seven to ten hours.

At this point, the reader might wonder why electric cars were popular at all. One reason for the temporary success of the electrics was their dependability compared to other types of autos. The steam car was difficult to get started and would sometimes run out of steam. The gasoline-powered car of 1900 seemed to be plagued by constant mechanical breakdown, and, as has been mentioned, was really still in the experimental stage. The dependable electrics, though slow, were also quiet and fumeless. If the owner just was not in a hurry, the electric was a pretty good automobile.

Around 1900, Thomas Edison, having faith in the future of electric locomotion, took a good hard look at the battery problem. He had been around batteries since the days when he was a telegraph operator. Every telegraph office had its battery room and young Tom Edison often experimented with the batteries when message activity was light and he had a little spare time. In later years, in his own laboratories, batteries were standard equipment. It was Edison's feeling that the lead-acid type of battery by its very nature was self-destructive, and a better type was needed.

Putting himself and some of his best men on the project, the inventor began a task that was to become one of the most difficult he had ever undertaken. He was determined to make an alkaline battery — one that would not be self-destructive. Some twenty thousand experiments were required just to discover what metals would best function in an alkaline solution.

During the years of experimentation, one step in the process was to test the batteries under actual driving conditions. The Stanhope-Locomobile was loaded with a set of cells, then driven on a circular route through communities surrounding West Orange. The rougher the roads the better as far as Edison was concerned.

It was not until 1908, after fifty thousand experiments had been conducted, that Edison put nickel-iron aklaline batteries into full production. Their use was not restricted to electric cars. Thousands were made for electric trucks, mine locomotives, miners' cap lamps, passenger car lighting and air-conditioning, as well as for emergency current for railroad signal systems. Twenty-five cells on exhibit in Building 6 of the Mu-

seum were used for more than 25 years on the Southern
Pacific Railroad — the alkaline cells in some operations
seemed almost indestructible.

Although still manufactured for most of the above-
mentioned uses, the battery no longer powers cars. The
electric passenger vehicle in the United States went out
of style about forty-five years ago, though electric
trucks were in use through the early 1940's.* The alkaline battery could neither increase the speed nor reduce
the frequency of recharging operations to any great
extent. For these reasons, the electrics gave way to the
faster gasoline-powered cars that could be refueled in
minutes. Before the faster cars completely took over,
however, many thousands of people were to own and
use electric cars. Just between 1896 and 1915, 35,000
electrics were built in the United States alone, and the
Edisons were among those that purchased several of
them.

The other two electric cars at the Museum were used
by Mrs. Edison. They can be found in Building 4 along
with the Model T, the only exhibits in that building.
Both are Detroit Electrics made by the Anderson Carriage Company. The older of the two is an open car
called the Victoria, built in 1911, while the newer enclosed model is a Brougham, 1914 vintage. The latter

---

*At the time of this writing, car manufacturers and inventors
(using knowledges and techniques developed in the last twenty
years) are producing new experimental electric vehicles without
the shortcomings of the earlier electric cars. They may go into
mass production soon.

car bears some resemblance to the Victoria, in that it has battery storage space in front and back (where the engine and luggage spaces are found in modern cars), has a tiller rather than a steering wheel, is without a windshield wiper, and carries the motor in the middle of the frame directly under the passenger space. There the resemblance ends. The Brougham was a much more expensive car, being fully enclosed in a metal body. One cushioned seat, well upholstered, provided space for the driver and passengers. This seat was in the back of the enclosed part, so that a space of about four feet separated the driver from the windshield. Diagonally opposite the driver was a bucket seat for an additional passenger. By depressing a small lever beneath the seat, the passenger could swivel completely around and face the driver. In the late 1960's, a few car manufacturers reintroduced this novelty in modern vehicles.

Although Edison took an interest in cars, particularly open ones, he evidently left the driving to others. Like many other drivers of his day, he had concerns about the safety of automobiles. The early glass windshields, before the use of shatter-proof glass and safety belts, were the cause of many injuries in collisions. Steering apparatus was often faulty, and Edison was constantly on the lookout for stronger steering columns. His son Theodore remembers his father, during the course of a trip, buying a car from its owner right on the spot because it had a husky steering mechanism.

A well-verified story told about the inventor relates that as he approached the age of 70 he finally decided to teach himself to drive. He thereupon took out the 1914 Brougham, got going too fast down a rather steep hill and ended up in a ditch. Unhurt, but unable to move the vehicle from its muddy bed, he finally gave up in disgust and walked back to his home, making a special point to avoid everyone. The family and servants, not wanting to risk his wrath, avoided the subject of the missing car for the rest of the day, but when darkness approached they decided that everyone must spread out on nearby roads to try to find the Detroit Electric. The search proved successful.

The most recent car at the Museum, the Ford Model T, carried the inventor between his home and his laboratory. It is a five-passenger black touring car with an adjustable windshield, a folding top, and imitation leather upholstery. The vacuum windshield wiper is suspended from the top of the windshield rather than from the bottom as in modern cars. A small finger-lever provided for its manual operation when power failed, and a dangling crank at the front of the car was available for turning the engine over in case the electric self-starter failed to function.

The self-starter was invented in 1911 by Charles Kettering, and it was one of the improvements in gas-powered vehicles that helped to increase the popularity of such cars, making them much easier to operate.

The Ford Model T was an important car in its day, and in no small way made the nation motor-car minded. Between 1908 and 1927, fifteen million Model T's were produced and sold at prices that the average family could afford.

Edison's use of Model T's showed practicality, but was also an indication of his close relationship with the Model T's creator, Henry Ford. It was Edison who encouraged Ford to go ahead with the internal combustion engine when Ford, much discouraged, was facing great obstacles. Ford never forgot Edison's words of encouragement, and they may have been responsible for his tendency in later life to declare, "It's always too soon to quit!"

One end of the machine shop showing two lathes in the foreground
and the Holyoke elevator in the background to the left.

10

The Machine Shop

THE MAJOR INVENTIONS developed by Thomas Edison were not actually constructed by him, but came from the skilled hands of his master craftsmen. Edison conceived the idea and then thought it through to the stage where a plan was drawn up, but when an actual model was desired, he passed his plan to his mechanics.

The place where many of them worked was the machine shop, which can still be seen just as it was. This consists of two large rooms on two floors in Building 5. A visitor enters the ground-floor shop where the heaviest machinery is located, and is likely to be amazed by his first view of this large working area. A room filled with machinery, long shafts, thick leather belts, and blueprint racks, stretches out before him. Down the left side of the shop, a long workbench extends almost the entire length of the room. This is well fitted with heavy-duty vises every few feet. Big lead mallets and steel wrenches lie beneath goose-neck lamps, indicative of long hours of work performed here many years ago.

Opposite the workbench and to the right of the walkway, an orderly row of LeBlond lathes seem to block off the central portion of the shop to the right of the walkway. In this area are located various machines, from small drill presses to different types of grinders, shapers, cutting machines, and milling machines.

The heavy equipment is located in the center of the room. It includes two very large planers and one gigantic radial drill press. These were purchased in 1887 at a cost of about $3,000 each. Above them are the tracks for a movable hoist that is now located at the end of the room. On the far side of the shop are more machines of various sizes and shapes.

Visitors are sometimes curious as to why Edison had such large machinery in his shop considering that most of his inventions were small in size. Men who worked for him feel that it was the inventor's interest in mining and milling New Jersey ore that prompted his investment in such a large shop. In 1882 he had difficulty buying iron for his new dynamos at a reasonable price and toward the end of that decade he actually sent survey teams down the 800-mile length of the Appalachian Mountains taking samples of rock for iron content at regular intervals. By the early 1890's, he had acquired several thousand acres of ore-bearing land near Ogdensburg, New Jersey, and spent three million dollars there in a project which terminated in failure in 1899.

It seems that the Sault Sainte Marie Canal, which connected Lake Superior and Lake Huron, was deepened in the mid-1890's, making it possible for large iron-ore-filled ships to transport twice the tonnage of ore previously carried. The price of ore in Ohio and Pennsylvania dropped from $6.50 to $3.50 per ton. Even though Edison's methods had reduced the price of Jersey iron, it could not now compete with the higher grade and lower priced ore from the Mesabi fields in Minnesota.

The largest steam shovel in the world was obtained by the inventor and it moved thousands of tons of ore into an elaborate conveyor belt system that carried the material to giant crushing machines. These had been designed and made at the West Orange Laboratory. One of them that Edison called the "Giant Rolls" was among the largest steam-powered crushers ever constructed.

At the far end of the shop is an open freight elevator with a gate of wooden bars. A sign on the gate states in large black letters: "For the Use of Mr. Edison Only." The elevator was manufactured by the Holyoke Machine Company in 1887 and installed the year the laboratory opened. The truth is that for most of the 44 years of the laboratory's operation, Edison did not use the elevator. On his daily tours to check on the progress of his employees, he used the stairs in going from one floor to another. The elevator, he said, was too slow.

About 1926, with age starting to take its toll on the inventor, the men in the shop agreed to reserve the elevator for "the old man," as they affectionately referred to him. If it was needed to move freight or machinery, the men would wait until Edison had gone through the shop. He balked at the idea at first, but then reluctantly agreed, sensing the wisdom of their concern.

The power for all of the equipment originally came from a steam engine, because electric motors were still not well developed. In 1910, however, two large DC electric motors were installed on a platform over the obsolete steam engine. The means of conveying the power to the machines was mechanical, and it still remains so today. That is to say, the electric energy was used to turn two large shafts, one on each side of the room and suspended just below the ceiling. Large leather belts connect the shafts to their respective motors as well as to each of the machines. When one of the shafts revolves, each of the machines that is connected and engaged by belt with the shaft also runs. From the late 1700's to the early 1900's, factories that relied on steam or water power used this type of mechanical power system.

Not far from the elevator is the access window to the stock room. Here, Edison's workmen had at their disposal a variety of materials and tools including animal, vegetable, and mineral matter which they could experiment with as they sought parts and pieces for new inventions. Edison referred to his stock room as his "junk pile," claiming that any successful inventor had to have such a collection to insure that his men would have everything they needed to make inventions.

Some of the items can be seen today, for instance, elephant hide, walrus hide, whalebone, vegetable ivory, a block of felt, and a large turtle shell, plus all sorts of metal stock, and tools. Edison's "junk pile" reflects one of the reasons his laboratory was unique — a real "invention factory" where lack of equipment would never hinder the rapid progress being made.

Edison and his laboratory staff in 1893. The inventor is seated in the center of the front row, with W. K. L. Dickson, his principal aide in the development of the motion picture camera, third from the right in the second row.

A view of the Library as seen from the first balcony. Some of the 10,000 books are plainly visible. The famous clock and the Silvette painting are on the far wall, not more than a few feet from Edison's "workbench" or desk which is at the bottom of the picture.

11

The Library

A SONG LONG POPULAR on the American scene, *Grand-father's Clock*, by Henry C. Work has this refrain:
    ... "But it stopped, short, never to go again,
        When the old man died."

The composer probably had never heard of Edison, but 55 years later some interesting parallels developed between the lyrics and the passing of the inventor. In 1931 Edison was a grandfather; he was nicknamed the "old man," he had a clock about as tall as he was, and the clock stopped when the "old man" died. At least that is the story.

The six-feet-in-diameter timepiece was built into the wall of Edison's office, called the library, in a panel of oak, carefully carved with ornate branches and leaves. Presented to Edison by his employees on the occasion of his 42nd birthday, the clock kept time until the morning of Edison's death. It would seem that almost at the very moment his life ebbed away, the clock mysteriously came to a halt — 3:27 A.M. October 18, 1931. Although an investigation was later made into this strange coincidence, the actual reason for the clock's stopping has never been established. It would almost appear, however, that even time was under the control of this master inventor. Left undisturbed, this famous clock may be seen by visitors as they view this spacious room, one of the highlights of the laboratory tour.

Furnished throughout in yellow pine, the library is a room about fifty feet square with two balconies, the lower one lining three sides, and the upper balcony, four sides of the room. These are reached by a narrow stairway at one corner, and contain book cases arranged at right angles to the wall and railing thereby making small alcoves for study and research. Underneath the first balcony are similar book cases and cabinets.

About 10,000 books are in the library, the major part of a collection that Edison began gathering when he was a telegraph operator in Louisville, Kentucky. Among these early acquisitions was a set of 27 volumes of the *North American Review,* a scientific magazine which he purchased for two dollars. He was carrying part of this set in a sack slung over his shoulder as he walked to his rooming house following his tour of duty on the midnight shift. It was 3 A.M. and a policeman, thinking he had a thief in sight, yelled to young Edison to stop. But Edison, who was almost deaf, did not hear the officer and only realized what was going on when he became aware of someone shooting at him. Fortunately, the policeman was a poor shot and the matter was soon straightened out. Edison made it to his rooming house, and those very same books are now on a shelf in a first floor alcove.

Many of the other books on that floor contain records of inventions made in Europe. France and Germany are nations whose scientific achievements have been particularly noteworthy; therefore some of the major sets of volumes in the library deal with inventions made in those countries. In addition, there are hundreds of other volumes dealing with everything from geologic surveys of the United States to the history of Europe in the 19th century. Most of the books, however, are in the scientific field.

Edison's use of these books can best be summed up in the words of the inventor himself as he spoke to a visitor:

> When I want to discover something, I begin by reading up everything that has been done along that line in the past — that's what all these books in the library are for. I see what has been accomplished at great labor and expense in the past. I gather the data of many thousands of experiments as a starting point, and then I make thousands more.

The balconies contain books and back issues of many magazines as well as an extensive bottled ore collection from Edison's iron mining days, letter boxes, ledgers and reports of the Edison Company, maps and atlases, plus assorted other things too numerous to mention here.

The center portion of the library is open from floor to ceiling, a distance of 28 feet, and four multiple-light chandeliers are suspended from the ceiling. These lights, with others in the alcoves, are all on when visitors enter this beautiful room. The reflection of the light from the yellow pine woodwork gives the room a bright golden glow. And then everywhere are pictures — most of them are of famous men Edison knew: presidents, industrialists, naturalists, inventors. There are also pictures of electric trains and trucks powered with Edison batteries; pictures of factory installations and previous labs and workshops.

Near the center of this room is Edison's rolltop desk. He called it his workbench, nostalgically remembering those earlier days at Newark and Menlo Park when much of his time was actually spent in the workshops with his men. During the later years at West Orange, however, the inventor was more and more at this desk, receiving reports from capable lieutenants in the specialty labs and machine shops that had sprung up around the laboratory buildings. Assisting the inventor was his able secretary of many years — W. H. Meadowcroft. His desk remains in a large alcove of the library.

Edison's desk was closed and sealed a few hours after his death on that fateful October morning by his son Charles. No one saw the interior of that desk for the following 16 years, but in February, 1947, almost on the day that Edison would have been 100 years of

Edison at his roll-top desk in 1914. Today the desk still stands in the Library, its cubbyholes filled with the paraphernalia the inventor left there in 1931.

age, a ceremony took place in the library. The details of it were broadcast from coast to coast. With distinguished guests, old-time employees, members of the Edison family, and representatives of the press and radio crowding around, Charles Edison opened the long closed desk, carefully took a few papers from the crowded cubbyholes and divulged their contents to the nation. Nothing earth-shaking was found but since that time the desk has remained open that visitors may see it just as Edison left it.

Paperweights, two or three bottles of strange chemical solutions, two phonograph arms and reproducers, assorted incoming letters, a bottle of Carissa Jelly made by a Mrs. Stevens on July 10, 1928, Listerine Antiseptic, a few photographs, some soda-mint tablets, cubbyholes jammed with notes, reports, memoranda, faded pictures, and stale cigars — all and more can be seen in Edison's desk. All suggest that the "Wizard" might be returning on the morrow.

The cigars remind us of one of Edison's habits — cigar smoking. Those who knew him say he smoked 15 to 20 cigars per day. Occasionally he chewed tobacco. Yet, almost stranger than fiction, the inventor would not allow cigarettes to be smoked anywhere in the laboratory. It was not the fire danger he was concerned about. As early as 1914, the inventor had made tests on cigarettes and as a result became convinced that cigarette smoking injured the brain. A special notice still taped to the inside of the glass on the time clock in the hall threatens dismissal to anyone caught smoking cigarettes.

Edison's sleeping habits were also unorthodox. As a young telegraph operator, he had learned the value of taking short naps, thereby extending the actual hours he could work and experiment. Edison discovered that six to eight hours of sleep at night was no longer necessary if short naps were taken whenever fatigue overtook him. He continued this practice throughout his adult life, and it is known that he had the peculiar ability to sleep anyplace — on the floor, on a table, on a pile of coal, or even in a rolltop desk! Some who worked with Edison report that he could go to sleep almost instantly, and upon waking 20 or 30 minutes later, would return to his work just as if he had not stopped.

At times, Edison was found napping by visiting dignitaries and often had to be roused from an undignified sleeping spot. When Mrs. Edison learned about her husband's practice of sleeping in odd places in the library, she had a cot moved into one of the alcoves and suggested firmly that he use it.

Directly under the clock is a painting of Edison in a Napoleonic pose, a tired expression on his face, and contemplating his improved 1888 phonograph, which is on a table before him. Ellis M. Silvette did the painting from an actual photograph of Edison taken after he and aids had worked steadily for 72 hours trying to perfect this invention so it could be shipped on a certain steamer to Europe. The machine was to be exhibited in the Crystal Palace at London. Like the determined French general, Edison hated to give up.

Edison left his library and laboratory for the last time on the morning of October 21, 1931. Although he died at home, his body laid in state in the library for two and one-half days where thousands came to see their great benefactor.

Edison's body was carried out to its final resting place 52 years to the day after his first successful incandescent lamp burned out at Menlo Park. During his lifetime he had been the recipient of over one thousand patents, and the creator of over six hundred separate inventions, more than any other person had accomplished in the history of the world.

The West Orange Laboratory remains a monument to the genius and creative energy of Thomas Edison and his loyal staff, while daily the people of the civilized world utilize the products of his fertile mind.

Tours and Visiting Hours

The Thomas A. Edison Laboratory was presented to the National Park Service in 1956, and was officially designated the Edison National Historic Site in 1962. The buildings are open all year, daily, except Christmas and New Year's Day. Visiting hours are from 9:30 A.M. to 4:30 P.M. Visitors are taken on tours by especially trained National Park Service personnel. Groups are welcome but reservations must be made in advance. The fee is 50 cents for all persons over the age of 15. School groups are free.

Visitors coming from the North, East, or South, can best reach the Site by driving via the Garden State Parkway. See the map below for more detailed instructions.

DIRECTIONS:

Driving South on Parkway, go off at Exit 147, Springdale Ave., and turn right on Park Ave.

Driving North on Parkway, go off at Exit 145, Oranges & Newark, drive to Park Ave. on margin road. Turn left on Park Ave.

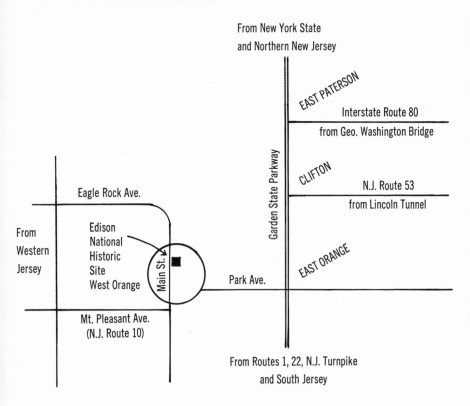

Bibliography

Bryan, George S., *Edison, The Man and His Work,* Garden City: Garden City Publishing Company, Inc., 1926.

Dickson, W. K. L. and Dickson, Antonia, *The Life and Inventions of Thomas Alva Edison,* New York: Thomas Y. Crowell and Company, 1894.

Dyer, Frank, Martin, Thomas M., Meadowcroft, W. H., *Edison, His Life and Inventions,* in Two Volumes, New York: Harper and Brothers Publishers, 1929.

Jehl, Francis, *Menlo Park Reminiscences,* Dearborn: Edison Institute, 1937.

Josephson, Matthew, *Edison,* New York: McGraw-Hill Book Company, Inc., 1959.

Lewis, Floyd H., *The Incandescent Light,* New York: Shorewood Publishers, Inc., 1961.

Nerney, Mary Childs, *Thomas A. Edison, A Modern Olympian,* Harrison Smith and Robert Haas, Inc., 1934.

Quigley, Martin, Jr., *Magic Shadows,* Washington, D.C.: Georgetown University Press, 1948.

Ramsaye, Terry, *A Million and One Nights,* New York: Simon and Schuster, 1926.

Read, Oliver, and Welch, Walter L., *From Tin Foil to Stereo,* New York: Howard W. Sams and Company, Inc., 1959.

Runes, Dagobert D., Ed., *The Diary and Sundry Observations of Thomas Alva Edison,* New York: Greenwood Press, Publishers, 1968.

Simonds, William A., *Edison, His Life, His Work, His Genius,* New York: The Bobbs-Merrill Company, 1934.

Tate, Alfred O., *Edison's Open Door,* New York: E. P. Dutton and Company, 1938.

PUBLICATIONS WRITTEN EXPRESSLY
FOR CHILDREN

Cousins, Margaret, *The Story of Thomas Alva Edison,* New York: Random House, 1965.

North, Sterling, *Young Thomas Edison,* Boston: Houghton Mifflin Company, 1958.

Palmer, Arthur J., *Edison, Inspiration to Youth,* West Orange: Edison Birthplace Association, Inc., 1959.

Index

Acoustic Telegraph (see Telegraph)

Amberol Record (see Record)

Anderson Carriage Co., 68

Anderson, William, 62

Ansonia, Conn., 42

Appalachian Mtns., 74

Arc lighting, 42

Armat, Thomas, 57

Automobile, Electric, 64, 65-70
Gasoline engine, 65-66, 70-71
Steam, 66

Baggage car laboratory, 12, 14

Bamboo filament lamp (see Electric light)

Barker, Professor George F., 42

Batchelor, Charles, 43

Battery (see Storage battery)

Bell, Alexander Graham, 38-40

"Black Maria," 59-63

Books (in library), 80-82

Boston, Mass., 14, 21, 25

Broadway Kinetoscope Parlor, 57-58

Brokerage houses, 22-25

Bronx, N.Y., 63

Buffalo Bill (see Cody, William F.)

Camera, Motion picture, 49-55

Carbon Button transmitter, 39-40

Chicago Exposition of 1893, 57

Clock, Library in West Orange, 79-80, 85

Cody, William F., 62

Columbia, S. S., 45

Corbett, James, 62

Cylinder phonograph (see
    Phonograph)
Cylinder, Movie, 52-53
Crystal Palace, 85

Da Vinci, Leonardo, 10
Desk, Edison's (West Orange),
    82-84
Detroit Electric Auto, 68-70
Dickson, W. K. L., 54-55, 77
Disc record (see Record)
Dynamo, Edison, 45-47

Eastman, George, 53
Edison, Charles, 82-83
Edison, Mrs. Mina Miller,
    68
Edison, Theodore, 69
Edison, Thomas A.,
    childhood, 12, 14, 21-22
    death, 11, 59, 79-80, 82
    driving habits, 69-70
    education, 12, 22
    employees, 18, 29-32, 43,
        45, 54-55, 73, 75-76, 83
    handwriting, 21-22
    income, 24-25
    inventions,
        electric light, 9, 41-47
        gold indicator, 22-23
        motion picture camera,
            49-56
        multiplex, 25-26
        phonograph, 28-39
        quadruplex, 26-27
        repeating telegraph 27-28
        rubber project, 18, 20

        stock ticker, 22-25
        storage battery, 65-69
        universal stock printer, 25
        vote recorder, 22
    marriages, 49
    methods in inventing, 73-74
    mother, 22
    objectives in laboratory, 14-
        15
    paying taxes, 26
    sleep habits, 42, 84-85
    smoking habits, 84
    telegraph operator, 14, 21,
        22, 80-81, 84
Electric light, 9, 41-47
    arc lighting, 42
    central station, 47
    dynamos, 45-46, 66
    filament lamps, 41-45
        bamboo, 41, 44-45
        cotton thread, 43-44
        paper, 44

Film, Celluloid, 53
Ford, Henry, 71
Ford, Model T, 65, 70-71
Frankfurt, Germany, 39

Gannon, Frank, 62-63
Giant rolls (see Iron ore
    milling)
Gilmore, W. E., 62-63
Goldenrod, 18, 20
"Grandfather's Clock," 79

Holyoke Machine Co., 75

"Invention Factory" (see
    Laboratory)
Iron ore milling operations,
    9, 74-75

Jehl, Francis, 43-44
Josephson, Matthew, 26-27

Kettering, Charles, 70
Kinetographic camera, 53-55,
    59
Kinetoscope, 53, 56-58
Kinetoscope Company,
    57-58
Kruesi, John, 29-30, 32

Laboratory,
    Home chemical, 12
    Baggage car, 12, 14
    Menlo Park, 8, 14, 15, 27,
        43-44, 82, 85
    Newark, 22, 25, 82
    West Orange, Building I,
        13, 16, 21, 32-35, 37,
        45-46, 50, 52-53, 56, 65
    Building II, 11, 16, 17-20,
        48
    Building III, 16
    Building IV, 16, 68
    Building V, 15, 41, 73-86
    Building VI, 15, 22, 67
    Blacksmith's shop, 16
    Library, 41, 78, 79-86
    Machine shop, 15, 72,
        73-77
    Music room, 15

    Stock room, 15, 76-77
Laboratory, First modern in-
    dustrial research, 15
Laboratory, Invention factory,
    10, 77
Lefferts, Marshall, 24-25
Light, Incandescent (see
    Edison, light)
Lighting, Arc (see Arc light-
    ing)
London, England, 58, 85
"Long-waisted Mary-Ann,"
    45, 46

Machine shop (see Laboratory,
    Machine shop)
Marey, E. J., 51
Meadowcroft, W. H., 82
Menlo Park Laboratory (see
    Laboratory, Menlo Park)
Milan, Ohio, 12
Morning-glory horn, 33
Morse, Samuel F. B., 28, 39
Morse code, 28
Muybridge, Edward, 51-52

Napoleon, 85
National Park System, 10, 87
Newark, N.J., 14, 22, 25, 26,
    29, 38, 82
New York City, 14, 32, 38, 39,
    45
North American Review, 80

Oakley, Annie, 62
Ogdensburg, N.J., 74-75
Orton, William, 38-39

Paris, 58
Paris Exposition (1889), 55
Pearl St. Electric Power Station, 47
Pennsylvania Railroad, 44
Pennsylvania, University of, 42
Phenakistoscope, 50
Philadelphia, 38, 39-40
Phonograph, 28, 29-36, 49-50
    Concert model, 34
    Edison home model, 33, 35
    Original model, 28-32
    Tinfoil, (see Original model)
    Type M, 33
Plateau, 50
Port Huron, Mich., 12, 22
Projection, Movie, 56-58

Roff, Norman C., 57
Ramsaye, Terry, 54, 62
Records, Cylinder
    Tinfoil, 30-33
    Blue Amberol, 33
    Wax (2 min.), 33-34
Records, Disc, 13, 18-19, 27-28, 34
Reis, J. P. (telephone), 39

Saint Louis World's Fair (1904), 47
San Francisco, 45
Scientific-American (magazine), 32
Silvette, Ellis, 85
Southern Pacific Railroad, 68
Stanhope-Locomobile auto, 65, 67

Stock room (machine shop), 15, 76-77
Stock ticker, 14, 22-25
Storage battery
    Lead-acid, 66, 67
    Nickel-iron alkaline, 67-68
Studio, First Motion Picture, 59-63

Telegraph, Acoustic, 38-39
    Multiplex, 25
    Quodruplex, 26-27
    Repeating, 27-28
Telephone, 37-40
Tinfoil phonograph, (see Phonograph)
Tobacco, Edison's use of, 84
Transmitter, Carbon Button, 39-40

Unison-stop device, 24-25
Universal Stock Printer, 25
Upton, Francis, 43, 45

Vision, Persistence of, 51
Vote recorder, Electric, 22, 23, 24

Western Union Telegraph Co., 24, 27, 38
West Orange laboratory (see Laboratory, West Orange)
Wolfe, J. A., 37
Wyoming, 42

Zoetrope, 50-51